The Philosophy of
NUMBERS

THEIR TONE AND COLORS

VOLUME II

A SMALL GEM
BY
MRS. L. DOW BALLIETT

Some Other Titles From New Falcon Publications

Aha! The Sevenfold Mystery of the Ineffable Love —Aleister Crowley
Aleister Crowley and the Treasure House of Images
—J.F.C. Fuller, Aleister Crowley, Lon Milo DuQuette and Nancy Wasserman
Aleister Crowley's Illustrated Goetia, Sex Magic, Tantra & Tarot:
An Insider's Guide to Robert Anton Wilson —Eric Wagner
Ask Baba Lon —Lon Milo DuQuette
Bio-Etheric Healing —Trudy Lanitis
Diary of the Antichrist —David Cheribum
Enochian Sex Magic and How To Workbook
—Aleister Crowley, Lon Milo DuQuette and Christopher S. Hyatt, Ph.D.
Enochian World of Aleister Crowley —DuQuette and Aleister Crowley
Info-Psychology, Neuropolitique, The Game of Life, What Does WoMan Want?
—Timothy Leary, Ph.D.
Nonlocal Nature: The Eight Circuits of Consciousness —James A. Heffernan
on What is —Ja Wallin
Pacts With The Devil, Urban Voodoo: A Beginner's Guide to Afro-Caribbean Magic
—Jason Black and Christopher S. Hyatt, Ph.D.
Rebellion, Revolution and Religiousness —Osho
Rebels & Devils; The Psychology of Liberation—Edited by Christopher S. Hyatt, Ph.D.
Reichian Therapy: A Practical Guide for Home Use —Dr. Jack Willis
Shaping Formless Fire, Seizing Power, Taking Power
Secrets of Western Tantra: The Sexuality of the Middle Path
Dogma Daze —Christopher S. Hyatt, Ph.D.
Steamo Goes to Havana, The Social Epidemic of Child Abuse
—Michael Miller, M.Ed., M.S., Ph.D.
The Illuminati Conspiracy: The Sapiens System —Donald Holmes, M.D.
The Magick In The Music and Other Essays —Stephen Mace
The Psychopath's Bible —Christopher S. Hyatt, Ph.D., and Jack Willis
The Secret Inner Order Rituals of the Golden Dawn —Pat Zalewski
The Way of the Secret Lover Taboo: Sex, Religion & Magick
—C. Hyatt, Ph.D., and Lon DuQuette
The Why, Who, and What of Existence —Vlad Korbel
Undoing Yourself With Energized Meditation and Other Devices
Woman's Orgasm: A Guide to Sexual Satisfaction
—Benjamin Graber M.D., and Georgia Kline-Graber, R.N.

Other Titles by J. Marvin Spiegelman, Ph.D

A Modern Jew in Search of Soul
Buddhism and Jungian Psychology
Catholicism and Jungian Psychology
Hinduism and Jungian Psychology
Mysticism, Psychology and Oedipus - A Small Gem
Protestanism and Jungian Psychology
Psychotherapy and Religion at the Millennium and Beyond
Psychotherapy as a Mutual Process
Reich, Jung, Regardie & Me - The Unhealed Healer
Rider, Haggard, Henry Miller & I - The Unpublished Writer
Sufism, Islam and Jungian Psychology
The Knight - A Small Gem
The Nymphomaniac
The Quest - Further Adventures in the Unconscious
The Tree of Life - Paths in Jungian Individuation
The Wisdom of J. Marvin Speigelman Vol. I - Selected Writings
The Wisdom of J. Marvin Speigelman Vol. II - Psychology and Religion

Other Titles by Dr. Israel Regardie

A Garden of Pomegranates
A Practical Guide to Geomantic Divination - A Small Gem
Attract and Use Healing Energy - A Small Gem
Be Yourself - A Guide to Relaxation and Health
Ceremonial Magic
Dr. Israel Regardie's Definitive Work on Aleister Crowley,
  The Eye In The Triangle
Healing Energy, Prayer and Relaxation
How To Make and Use Talismans - A Small Gem
Israel Regardie's The Foundations of Practical Magick
My Rosicrucian Adventure
Mysticism, Psychology and Oedipus - A Small Gem
Practical Magick - A Small Gem
Teachers of Fulfillment
The Art and Meaning of Magic - A Small Gem
The Body-Mind Connection, A Path to Well-Being - A Small Gem
The Complete Golden Dawn System of Magic
The Complete Golden Dawn System of Magic Book 1 - Ltd. Edition
The Complete Golden Dawn System of Magic Book 2 - Ltd. Edition
The Complete Golden Dawn System of Magic - The Black Edition
The Eye in the Triangle: An Interpretation of Aleister Crowley
The Golden Dawn Audio CDs, Vol. 1, Vol. 2, and Vol. 3
The Legend of Aleister Crowley
The Magic of Israel Regardie
The Middle Pillar
The Philosopher's Stone
The Portable Complete Golden Dawn System of Magic
The Tree of Life
The Wisdom of Israel Regardie - Vol. I
  Selected Introductions, Prefaces and Forewords
The Wisdom of Israel Regardie - Vol. II
  Selected Essays and Commentaries
The Wisdom of Israel Regardie - Vol. III
  Selected Articles, Introductions, Prefaces and Forewords
What You Should Know About the Golden Dawn
Wilhelm Reich, His Theory And Techniques
Aha! (Dr. Israel Regardie and Aleister Crowley)
Roll Away The Stone/The Herb Dangerous
  (Dr. Israel Regardie and Aleister Crowley)

MANY OF OUR TITLES AVAILABLE ON KINDLE!
Please visit our website at http://www.newfalcon.com

Copyright © 2023 New Falcon Publications

All rights reserved. No part of this book,
in part or in whole, may be reproduced, transmitted,
or utilized, in any form or by any means, electronic or mechanical,
including photocopying, recording, or by any information storage
and retrieval system, without permission in writing
from the publisher, except for brief quotations
in critical articles, books and reviews.

ISBN 13: 978-156184-253-7
ISBN 10: 1-56184-253-2

New Falcon Publications First Edition 2023

The paper used in this publication meets the minimum requirements
of the American National Standard for Permanence of
Paper for Printed Library Materials Z39.48-1984

Printed in USA

NEW FALCON PUBLICATIONS
2046 Hillhurst Avenue
Los Angeles, California 90027
www.newfalcon.com
email: info@newfalcon.com

The Philosophy of
NUMBERS

THEIR TONE AND COLORS

VOLUME II

A SMALL GEM
BY
MRS. L. DOW BALLIETT

NEW FALCON PUBLICATIONS
Los Angeles, California U.S.A.

VOLUME II

Contents

CHAPTER		PAGE
	Preface	1
1.	What Have I Been Doing in the Past?	3
2.	The Music of the Trees	7
3.	Of What Practical Use Are Colors and Notes?	11
4.	The Spiritual Birthday	15
5.	Colors and Their Individual Meaning	21
6.	To Find the Controlling Color in Your Number	23
7.	How to Find Your Life Song	27
8.	The Esoteric Value of Numbers	31
9.	Money–Its Vibration	33
10.	The Esoteric Value of Gems	35
11.	Furnishing Rooms in Their Own Colors	39
12.	The Colors and the Possibilities of the States and the Character of the People They Attract	43
13.	States That Vibrate 1–Idaho, Michigan, Rhode Island, Connecticut, District of Columbia, North Dakota, Indian Territory	45
14.	The State That Vibrates 2–Nevada	49
15.	States That Vibrate 3–Iowa, New York, South Carolina, West Virginia, New Mexico, Arizona	51
16.	States That Vibrate 4–Alabama, Mississippi, New Hampshire, North Carolina, Washington, Oklahoma	55
17.	The 5 Vibration–Utah	59
18.	States That Vibrate 6–Delaware, Massachusetts, Missouri, Montana, Texas, Maine	61
19.	States That Vibrate 7–California, Dakota, Maryland, New Jersey, Tennessee, Wyoming	65
20.	States That Vibrate 8–Georgia, Nebraska, Pennsylania, Vermont, Virginia, Wisconsin	69
21.	States That Vibrate 9–Alaska, Illinois	73
22.	States that Vibrate 11–Florida, Kansas, Kentucky, Louisiana, Minnesota, Ohio, Oregon, Colorado	75
23.	Our Island Possessions	83
24.	Find the Character of Different Parts of Cities/States	85

MRS. L. DOW BALLIETT

A MASTER OF VIBRATIONS AND NUMEROLOGY, FOUNDER OF THE
MASTER NUMBER SYSTEM, WHEREBY THE NUMBERS 11 AND 22 ARE
NOT REDUCED. MRS. BALLIETT COMBINED PYTHAGORAS' WORK
WITH BIBLICAL REFERENCE.

HER STUDENT, JUNO JORDAN, HELPED NUMEROLOGY BECOME THE
SYSTEM KNOWN TODAY AS PYTHAGOREAN. MANY NUMEROLOGISTS
TODAY STILL BASE THEIR WORK IN REFERENCE TO THESE WOMEN OF
THE CALIFORNIA INSTITUTE OF NUMERICAL RESEARCH.

This book is lovingly dedicated
to my niece
CAROLINA D. W. STILES
My life companion in search of truth and
my assistant in giving it expression.
–The Author

Preface

This book has been written in response to the requests of those who are interested in the study of Number Vibration. They came from all parts of the world asking for more of the simplified knowledge founded upon the one principal of Unity–that all things have but one source–and express in different forms the unity of the whole. The hidden strength or weakness of names, states, etc., as shown by the vowels have been evolved through the philosophy of numbers. From this source many unwritten laws can be made plain.

With greetings,
The Author.

CHAPTER I

What Have I Been Doing in the Past?

To find what you have been doing in the dim ages of the past, set to music the vibration of your name, find the harmonies and play them upon every instrument you can use. Hum the tune when alone; it has strange power and may open the door to past vibrations and make your body comprehend your soul's work. Also memorize and sing your birth number. Do not change the notes, as their order was chosen for your life teaching in this incarnation by your higher self. Repeat the motif in all possible ways.

We can see that musical instruments vibrate to certain numbers; judging with earth-bound eyes, we conclude that a person bearing the same vibration as an instrument has at some time in the past conquered the technique of that instrument or in some way been related to it. By means of the birth digit we know the place in the great choir the soul is now occupying.

If your name vibrates 11, you have the power to take any or every part in the great chorus, and yet your body will be so illy adjusted to the higher vibration, caused either by disobedience to the law of life or by loitering by the wayside, that you seem no more than a wreck. But all who possess the free numbers 8, 9, 11, or 22, are always greater than they seem.

The keynote of life is to be used to allow the soul to make the body a free channel of expression for the Spirit of the Divine. No vibration should be closed that leads to anything in earth, air, fire, or water, but hands, feet, tongue and thoughts should all be perfect vehicles of expression. The source within must be kept pure to allow the Trinity of Father, Son and Holy Spirit to possess your body. Then will you be kept in perfect health, and inasmuch as God rules, be able to control your environment. Otherwise you will become depleted in vitality by the division of self and suffer ill health and disease.

Let this prayer ever rule your mind, "Teach me, O Father, Son and Holy Spirit, thy spiritual law, and I will walk therein."

When one is out of harmony it is well to remember he stands somewhat in the same relation to the lower world that the head of a great corporation bears its employees. They may serve each other because it is fulfilling the law of equity, but they may lack the beauty of true art–the giving of that which has no price attached except that of love. All creatures look to you as you look up to God. Do not fail to give all things upon all planes a caress; it is their due and should be your pleasure. Also use the full gamut of sound when speaking; it is a message in tones to all creation.

CHAPTER 2

The Music of the Trees

Mrs. Childs, in letters from New York, says: "Every flower writes music in the air," and every tree that grows has a note sounding within its heart. Do you doubt it? Try the willow and the oak, the elm and the poplar, and see if each has not its own peculiar sound waiting only for the master's hand to evoke sweet music. One of the most remarkable instruments ever invented give proof of this.

M. Guzikaw was a Polish Jew, a shepherd in the service of a nobleman. From earliest boyhood music seemed to pervade his being.

As he tended his flocks in the lonely fields he was ever fashioning reeds and flutes from trees that grew around him. He soon discovered that the tones of his flutes varied according to the wood used. By degrees he came to know every tree by its sound, and the forests around him became to him an unawakened orchestra.

His skill in playing upon his rustic flutes attracted

attention. The nobility invited him to their houses, and he became a favorite of fortune as men never wearied of hearing him.

But soon his health failed and physicians told him he must give up the flute or die. It was a frightful sacrifice to ask, because music to him was life.

But his old familiarity with trees of the forest came to his aid. He took four rounded sticks and bound them together with bands of straw. Across these he arranged numerous pieces of round, smooth wood of different kinds. To the eye they seemed irregularly arranged, for some jutted beyond the straw foundation at one end and some at the other, in and out, in apparent confusion, the whole being fastened together with twine, as men lash rafts.

This instrument was laid on an ordinary table and struck with two ebony sticks. Rude as the instrument was Guzikow brought from it such rich and liquid melody that it seemed to take the heart of man on its winds and bear it aloft to the Throne of God. Those who have heard it describe it as far exceeding even the miraculous warblings of Paganini's violin.

The Emperor of Austria head it and forthwith took the Polish peasant into his own especial service.

Before this gifted being was placed a wooden table on which rested his rude looking instrument, which he touched with ebony sticks. At first the sound was only that of struck wood and the swelling of the orchestra completely drowned the voice, but gradually the wonderful instrument arose above all other sounds, clear, swelling, warbling like a nightingale. The orchestra arose higher and higher, but above all swelled the rich tone of the magic instrument, liquid and strong like the song of the skylark. Those who heard it listened in delighted wonder that the trees could be made to speak thus under the touch of Genius.

CHAPTER 3

Of What Practical Use Are Colors and Notes?

Anything to be of use must touch, at some point, the material plane of the individual. The force that produces the colors that environ a person is the force of activity called the soul, which is the eternal part and consequently the subjective or esoteric part. In order to unfold, the soul is largely dependent upon the body. The body, in turn, is dependent upon the strength or spiritual activity of the soul, which when properly attuned to body can reach into the unseen world close to the presence of the Creator, where is neither yesterday nor tomorrow, nothing but the eternal Now. The nearness of a soul to its creator depends entirely upon its growth, as it assimilated the higher spiritual meaning of an environment it has power to advance higher into the spiritual world. To this added strength the body must be attuned, like a good instrument, in order to be able to give true expression in the objective world. The body must harmonize all vibrations, called by men high and low, but in the upper realm, where the soul functions, there is neither high nor low, but every deed performed, when guided by the highest of which the individual is capable, is rewarded.

Every power the boundless soul contains must be met and harmonized before the perfect man is evolved. Men call Jesus the ideal man, and consciously or unconsciously, this is the goal toward which they are working. We aid the soul when we surround the body with harmonious environment.

When a pleasant event happens to you, remember that by good thoughts or deeds, sometime in the past, you have opened the channel for its reception. If the event is unpleasant, it is a friend come to show you some past weakness. Clear the earth plane of that vibration by making just recompense, then ascend to the soul plane with your account of money, pride or injustice and ask the God within you if the debt is fully paid. Do not refuse the lash. After this is done, ask the All Good to take it from your environment and it will go and never return. The sunshine of good will ever after use that channel to bring you peace and goodwill. This vibration will then ring out its note of joy and its color will be pure and bright.

To find the character of any event, great or small, get its vibration. For instance, suppose you have committed the sin of lying:

l vibrates to 3
i vibrates to 9
e vibrates to 5
———
17 = 8

The digit of lie is 8. 8 is a free number and to reach it in its fullness all channels of your being must be opened.

Its spiritual structure is expressed by the vowels e and i. The i means unbridled expression upon all planes, the e means the vibratory action of the mind. The esoteric colors of the letter are red and pink. When you clear the vibratory channel of the lie you make your red and pink glow with spiritual light and the canary color, which is the objective force which carried the lie to the outer world, hovers over you like a benediction, its note, in a manner, freed. When you have overcome, strike the note C–the keynote of 8–and let it vibrate its truth through your body. The opposite of lie, truth, vibrates to 6, and its note is A. This does not mean that 6 is true and 8 is false. It rather shows the strong vibration of 8 dares and expresses all things, and only from its internal strength can the fountain keep the outer streams clear and clean.

When the atmosphere of self seems to hang like a heavy pall about you, know that the soul desires the body to help it clear some vibration which has not been opened or which has become clogged by forces out of harmony with the Trinity of Body, Soul and Spirit.

Be perfectly sure if you had not attracted that which is present, you would not have it. If the soil is not prepared the seed cannot take root. No evil can approach you unless the evil within your own heart attract it. Do not repine or mourn; arise and face the obstacle. Find its vibration, its color, note and quality. Set about removing it with prayer and just action, making reparation where necessary, and you will clear the colors of your vibration. This can not be done effectively unless you work upon all planes of action. Do not shirk. Meet the emergency with courage. God has no needs, and when you realize yourself as only equal to your brother man, you then know what God means.

When this is done, find your life song. Sing, whistle and play it until you have mingled its notes with all the universe.

When the obstacle has been met and you have forgiven yourself and forgotten it, then its sting will be removed from the minds of others. So long as you keep it in mind and talk about it, its lesson has not been learned and it may return in another form. When you have made honest reparation to God and man, then forgive yourself.

CHAPTER 4
The Spiritual Birthday

Is it not well to think about the planes of Body, Soul and Spirit and their governing law? When in harmony, these planes act as one. Then the law of Spirit is present and grants the desires of the body and the Soul. When separated by inaction or false statements, the door of nature closes–and Man is under the task-master of his own will; the will is largely governing civilization today and from it few if any real masters are found. True, the last century was rich in scientific discoveries with its telegraphs and telephones but the race of men were not Spiritually uplifted. Commerce was benefitted; Souls were not advanced. The growth should begin in the Body, in the Soul and in the Spirit of man. When buildings are erected to teach the laws Jesus tried to teach His disciples to understand what are now the mysteries of Water, Fire, Air and Earth, and to manifest His dominion with them, then the race will advance; commerce will aid but not govern the human. Such laws can be taught scientifically when Body and Soul stand in equality.

The physical plane has demonstrated its mathematical laws so sure and accurate, the stars that arise a century hence are looked forward to with the same assurance as the morning sun. Man trifles with nature, but not nature with man. We in ignorance diverge, nature never. Man must go to nature for its aid. Nature does not come to man and yet in the visible world it is man's strongest friend. Electricity has always been present since creation's dawn, the same as when men made it a body so it could help him do his daily tasks. When he made instruments it could use, as head, hands and feet in the visible world, it willingly did the work of man. This was done upon the physical plane, where actions alone is the keynote. Nature will drown a man as quickly as it will cleanse him. It seems to have not motive; it simply acts when pockets are made for it to carry our goods in it carries them. Disputes of any kind cannot be settled definitely upon this plane. As it is devoid of motive, has only action, motives are found on the plane of soul. One must go there to find a regard for what caused the action. Here it is "an eye for an eye," a dollar for a dollar. When life seems unbearable, know you are functioning upon the physical plane, the plane of greatest inharmonies. Select from the things and persons about you such parts as are good, and you love, then practically move to the soul plane, where understandings are made. Leave the parts you cannot settle to the intelligence of the universe. You cannot move anything to this higher plane but what is rightfully your own and those things that will not injure any man can go with you. When you have done your part for the whole and not self alone, go above and trust the Universal Spirit of God. It will lead you to the soul plane, where happiness is born, and there sees in action upon the physical plane what you have set in motion, or your plans are not sane and are worthless. Those persons who will not move must fight it out below, and it should not trouble you, only when they ask for your help you should give it to them. All strength comes from above, so must soul and body meet when these two planes mingle. Spirit recognizes their harmony and grants their requests, but only in truth can they meet and blend. Nature cannot be ruled by will or coercion, only by thought through action. Such as the Messiah gave to it. How foolish seems the western world to close the door that leads to such a friend. When we go to Nature we are inclined to go for our bodies' sake rather than true communion with its mysteries. Since Nature's forces have been made useful man has become less spiritual. He should first train his own body and through its perfection the soul can act and show man greater things than he now dreams of. When the world awakes to the possibility of teaching spiritual truths upon all planes, as Jesus taught, we will have a race of masters proving the physical worth of Jesus, teaching outside of this vicarious atonement. Through sane development humanity can be lifted to a higher vibration. To do this, as a beginning we all can approach nature upon the simple plane of action, go to her and show her we recognize her presence by putting somewhere upon our bodies the color of the day; through this little act we can approach the Cosmos and justly expect its harmonious recognition.

Another way to begin is to recognize our *Spiritual Birthday*. In youth one's yearly birthday was an epoch of interest. If each birthday brought with it the same force as the one that was present the day of our birth, we would at no age forget its arrival; but it requires several years for the same force to return. There is held within the system of every month almost always three days that bear this same force as the present that brought you into the world. A child that was born March 1, 1883, will find his Spiritual Birthday in the Spirit force of the day, month and year he was born in.

Month vibrates   3
Day digit, vibrates 1
Year digit vibrates 2
              ―
              6

The Spiritual Birthday of this child, or any one else, is when the combination of month, day and year digit is 6. On that day the colors of scarlet, heliotrope and orange are in the atmosphere and are the vehicle for the note A. When the earth dust is made finer in our bodies we will see these colors with the outer eye on this day of all days that greets us with our own birth force. This child was born March 1, 1883, the same force will return on the 10th day, as it will be month 3, digit of day 1, digit of year 2. Add these, which result in 6. Also it returns on the 19th and 28th. This makes three days of importance in one month. These days are your days of training, the days to find just what your plan of life will reveal, for the same law is present in every month, day and year; find your own force in the same way.

For the first few months keep a record of these days, what they are filled with if your life has drifted into harmonious channels they will be happy; if not you must train them to what you deem best for everyone. By watching the events, feelings, pleasures and business you will see what your natural life work suggests; follow it out only make it what is brightest and best. If it shows amusements, encourage amusements of worth, begin by taking those with you your mind selects. When the cycle returns you will receive favors. This child will naturally fall into a part on a 6-day, a drive, an honor, a lot of callers and plenty of work–a busy, happy day will the 6th birthday be, and no unhappy feelings should find a place in your day of all days, because what you put into them the cycle returns to you. You will soon know what to expect upon this one day without disappointment. You can open any door your soul knows, you can meet and it appears to you on this day. Know it's your extended life to meet if new; if old troublesome thoughts or acts appear, turn them to pleasure. You must do it or nature will not help you if you do not help her as your natural mother.

What is valuable to man is to cultivate his own being into that which is everlasting and dwells in the Soul, and which is gained through action upon the physical plane, where all success of the hands depends upon borrowing Nature's forces. We must realize they are only the helpers to aid the true growth of being. A Soul cannot, throughout the great eternities, lose its Spiritual growth; it may at times be so enshrouded by unyielding flesh as to be rendered inactive, but it will again arise. We recognize the achievements of scientists in bringing animal and vegetable life into great perfection by putting the right combinations of species together and knowing how to borrow Nature's forces to perfect the work, but without constant action upon the plane of sight the animals and plants will return to their primitive conditions. While Being rises as the result of its growth, Nature returns to its original state.

CHAPTER 5

Colors and Their Individual Meaning

No. 1 Seeks to be a flame–a light in dark places and also at times acts as a consuming fire.

No. 2 Gold–seeks to express rest.

No. 3 Seeks to express any color or thing that presents itself. Should express 1 and 2.

No. 4 The blue seeks to express illumination and the green consciousness through intellect.

No. 5 Pink seeks to express power, life, refinement, harmony and a study of that region just beyond sight.

No. 6 Scarlet, heliotrope and orange seek to express wealth, rest and motion, knowledge and a forgetfulness of disdain.

No. 7 Brick and steel, seek to march and honor those who test the Trinity.

No. 8 Canary seeks to express mirth, space, charm, hope, zeal, religion, the highest.

No. 9 Red seeks to express light, stillness, love and not to impose upon the menial.

No. 11 White, black, yellow and violet seek to express wisdom, taste and to walk not with the odious.

No. 22 Cream, seeks to touch all things.

CHAPTER 6
To Find the Controlling Color In Your Number

The strongest color of any one's vibration is the one nearest the fountain of spirit found within the fit temple called the body. The soul, which is one with both the spirit and the body, is the builder of the body and through it sends out its vibrations and reveals them as colors to those whose eyes are attuned to the vibration of the finer forces. Others fell their presence, especially when there is a conflict of colors caused by the inharmony of the individual. When this occurs, and a weaving or dullness hangs over you like a mantle, take the control color of your vibration and realize it as the centre of your physical being and as the link which connects you with the great chain of love force which surrounds all things in God's embrace. Grasp the color firmly and reverently, and breathe from that point of your body just back of the stomach, known as the solar plexus, pushing out your color with will. Think of it as the offer of a friendly hand. Those who are vibrating the same color and force, will feel it when it reaches their environment.

Then take the next color and the next, pushing them out to the circumference of your wheel of life, never losing the presence of the stronger, until you bring their strength to the color of your birth vibration, which you should recognize as the color in which you are to find new strength. Keep your colors free from confusion–the higher the vibration the more strength it contains, and the more useful it is for all purposes of life. When its force is felt as peace, your vibration is at its highest and the desires of your soul are being met, and life on all planes of existence is being adjusted; not only for yourself, for when your desires shall be completely realized, the Universal Brotherhood of Man will be known, and you are now helping along the race by vibrating from within.

Individual life progresses in cycles of greater or less duration and these cycles are expressed by the numbers of the name and birth. The vowels in the name show the hidden strength not seen upon the objective side of life.

As an example we will make a chart for John Wanamaker, who was born July 11, 1838. He is dealing with the strong vibrations of objective and spiritual life and the desire of this brave soul is to win.

John vibrates to 2.

Wanamaker to 6, making the digit of his name 8.

July is the seventh month, the digit of the day is 11, the digit of the year is 2, making his birth number 9, 11.

Somewhere in past lives he won the lowest of the free vibrations 8, in some way overcoming the earth forces and getting a little of the soul yellow making canary.

This 8 is the vibration that understands the world and it needs as does no other. Canary is the strongest of John Wanamaker's colors and is the controlling point called the centre. The a or i in the vowel of his last name acts as flame of light illuminating even the weak points. His next important color is gold from the 2 of John. Then the heliotrope, scarlet and orange from the o of John and from Wanamaker.

When he gains any part of the strong vibrations of his birth numbers he will assimilate the force of character gained from 9 and 11, which numbers he chose through which to work his way through life. But his canary constantly covers him as a cloud.

The colors of his birth vibration, which he is trying to enter, are found in the outer circles. These are beneath him like a mighty ocean, over which he is trying to pass. (For particulars see "*Balliett's Success Through Vibration*.")

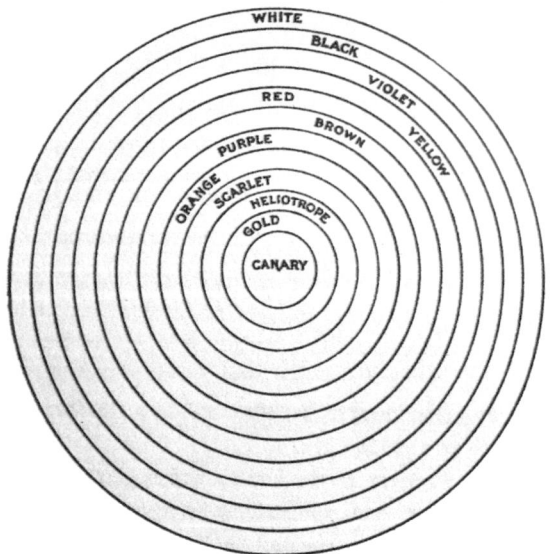

John Wanamaker's color scheme.
Born July 11, 1838.

A color scheme can be developed from one's own vibrations to be used in furnishing and dress.

CHAPTER 7
How To Find Your Life Song

If life is a state of activity and all things are vibrating, then each thing must have its own rate of motion and its own keynote, or else chaos and not law would result. Each individual incarnation may have a different keynote or birth vibration in which lies the unrealized desires the soul wishes to gain.

By complying with Nature's Laws you can vibrate to any musical key.

The strength of the key to which you are now vibrating was made somewhere in the past and the memories of its victories is stored in the soul and revealed to men by the letters used in the name. By individual letters of the name we catch glimpses of cycles made and strength stored.

Some brave soul boldly step out into the birth paths of whole octaves of sound–found in 11 and 22, which are vibrating to the octaves of C and D. When these are found in the birth-path and not in the name, always regard the bearer as an explorer in an unknown country to which he must adjust and harmonize himself or he will pass through life without his soul's approval and express an inharmonious environment.

There is no better teacher than the God within. Let your own soul teach you; trust it, and know the thing you need is under your hand. When you fulfill the objective law and do your best, the thing you desire for your highest good will come to you in many different ways. Do not confine yourself to any one route. If that you desire does not come, something just above it will take its place. Simply do your best.

There is no better way to open all the vibrations of the body than to take your own name and birth number and use them as found in the chart.

Your name holds for you the vibrations found in the past, within those boundaries were probably honors, riches and fame. Nothing but the victories of your incarnations are stored away, as only the acts of highest motive go into God's realm.

So when you strike the chords of harmony, or those which are not complete, know that only the best of your past experiences can come to you by means of harmonious tones.

Strike your own notes and let them vibrate through and through you, until closed brain cells are opened and memories of the past help you to reach higher planes in the present. Sing your birth song over and over until it becomes a well known path leading to your ideals.

CHAPTER 8
The Esoteric Value of Numbers

One contains the vowels o, e, which equal 11–the strongest of all forces.

Two contains the vowel o, which shows the maternal quality lying within; it contains a wealth of earth's highest colors.

Three contains the vowels e, e, of the value of 1– showing the spirit of three is in the creative of 1.

Four contains the vowels o, u, of the value of 9, showing the hidden strength of complete expression.

Five contains the vowels i, e, numerical value 5, it is the same objectivity as subjectivity, but contains the free vowel of 9, which stands as an incentive for free expression.

Six contains the vowel i, value 9–the esoteric side is higher than the objective–it calls for free expression in a limited realm.

Seven contains the vowels e, e, making 1. The sacred numbers 1, 3, and 7 are hidden flames of internal light.

Eight contains the vowels e, i, making 5; nine also contains this same esoteric vibration of 5. As eight and nine are free numbers, so the Christ body is present within the 8 and 9 lying unexpressed.

Eleven contains the vowels e, e, e, making 6. This number is made of two 3's, giving it the power to express on the objective plane the spiritual truths for which 11 stands.

Twenty-two contains the vowels 0, 3, of the value of 11–a high priest hidden deeply within waiting to be called forth.

CHAPTER 9
Money–It's Vibration

Money vibrates to 9–the vibration of the full, free expression of good or evil. 9 represents the soul-plane lying between matter and spirit ready to bring either into expression. Its vowels, which show the spiritual structure, are o, e,–their numerical value is 11. This is the highest of all vibrations. Every coin carries within its form hidden from mortal eyes this 11–the vibration of a righteous high priest. The inscription "In God we Trust" was not an accidental embellishment but the voice of the esoteric priest waiting to be brought forth. 9, which is the objective vibration of money, speaks more plainly for the brotherhood of man than any other vibration, and he who vibrates with it from a spiritual standpoint will have no needs.

Money, the great spiritual messenger, vibrates objectively to all shades of red and brown. Concealed within its form is violet, yellow, white and black. When its use is debased it lingers in the black corners of the world's vibration.

CHAPTER 10
The Esoteric Value of Gems

The spiritual strength of anything can be found by the vowels.

Many things, like individuals, seem unable to express the hidden strength of their true self. Others who are spiritually weak, are physically strong.

The following will show the objective and the esoteric value of a few gems:

No. 1 vibrates objectively to Moss-Agate and Aqua Marine.

Moss-Agate contains the vowels o, a, a, e; the digit of the vowels being 4. This number with the 1 expresses the Moss-Agate as a hidden flame of blue and green.

Aqua Marine vibrates objectively to 1. The vowels are a, u, a, in Aqua, vibrating 5, and a, i, e, in Marine, vibrating 6, making a total of 11. Esoterically the Aqua Marine is a triple flame of red and pink and contains the spiritual strength of 11.

No. 1 vibrates objectively to Turquoise. Its esoteric

value lies in u, u, o, i, e, which as a whole vibrates 8 or canary.

This gem holds hidden within itself the same color and character that the opal objectively expresses. It is rich in colors of red, yellow and pink. It is not a flame which means a light, but is rich in qualities belonging to the unseen side of life.

No. 3 vibrates to Amethyst and Ruby objectively. The esoteric value of the Amethyst a, e, shows it to be a pink flame of 6th vibration and to be related to orange, scarlet and heliotrope.

The Ruby is the same esoterically as objectively.

No. 4 vibrates to Emerald. The esoteric value is found in e, e, a, a double pink flame vibrating to the highest of all human vibrations, that of 11. It contains concealed within itself the spiritual accumulation of all jewels and expresses to the owner the strength of white, black, yellow or violet.

No. 6 vibrates to Diamond. Its esoteric value lies in i, a, o, making the 7th vibration, the number of a complete earth. It is a flame of free red fire together with orange, heliotrope and scarlet. This jewel holds within its flame the spiritual secrets of earth.

No. 7 vibrates to Agate. Its spiritual structure is shown in a, a, e, of 7 value. It vibrates the same upon the seen and unseen sides of life. It is a double pink flame and holds the possibilities of earth within its vibration.

No. 8 vibrates objectively to Opal. Its esoteric strength is found in o, a, 7, limited, complete earth vibration.

It expresses itself higher upon the seen than upon the unseen side of life, which may be a reason why it is sometimes considered a stone of ill omen. It lacks the hidden spiritual strength of some other jewels. Yet it is a flame of canary, heliotrope and scarlet and speaks upon the objective plane for a free body. It is mutely teaching Unity as it holds within itself these beautiful colors and sends them forth freely to the world seeking no return.

No. 8 vibrates to Beryl-Ligure. Its esoteric value lies in the vowels e, i, u, e, which make the high spiritual vibration of 22, holding within itself the power of organization and the elevation of the race. It is strong upon all planes. It is not a flame, but has hidden colors of red, pink and cream in abundance.

No. 11 vibrates objectively to Sapphire. Its hidden strength is not equal to its objective value. Its vowels a, i,e, give the numerical value of 6. This number shows the only trace of the physical found in this spiritual gem. It vibrates to all the colors in the objective gamut, and holds within a flame of red and pink.

No. 22 vibrates to Coral, but its esoteric value is only 7. It holds a hidden flame of cream, purple and mixed colors.

CHAPTER 11

Furnishing Rooms in Their Own Colors

Room No. 1 should be furnished in all shades of flame color. Select the many shades of harmonious color found in a flame of fire or light and blend them in the furnishing of this room. Remember that in a blue flame there are touches of silver.

Room No. 2 should be furnished in all shades of gold, from the lightest yellow to dark Tuscan gold. Let paper and furnishing be of mingled shades. The mystics say this is a color that evil can not penetrate.

No. 3 should express the colors best loved, or the colors of 1 and 2. No. 3 has no individual color vibration, but expresses whatever is present, whether harmony or the reverse, it should express a flame of gold.

Room No. 4 should be furnished in either blue or green or a harmony of both. The metallic colors also vibrate to this number.

Room No. 5 should be furnished in pink. It would be better to use the yellow pink shade, borrowing the orange from the vibration above, unless No. 4 is stronger in your environment, in which case use the blue pinks.

Room No. 6 should be furnished in scarlet, orange and heliotrope, all of them, or the one loved best.

Scarlet is most vital, orange is the color of power, and heliotrope is the color that shows glimpses of the life beyond sight to those prepared for the vision.

Room No. 7 should be furnished in the shades of brick, magenta, purple or steel. Choose from them silver gray and the shades of Italian red found in brick.

Room No. 8 should be furnished in canary. As this is a free number it can also claim white, which can be added to furnishing, decoration or wood-work.

Room No. 9 should be furnished in all shades of red and brown. Being a free number it also claims white.

No. 22 should be furnished in cream and white, but can take any of the 11 colors.

Room No. 11 should be furnished in violet, yellow, black and white. It can use any shade of these colors, or in fact, can use any colors of any of the vibrations.

You may expect strong events of all kinds in rooms 8, 9, 11, 22, as they possess strong vibrations. They will attract strong persons and it will be difficult to separate people who have occupied them for any length of time. Great joy and happiness will be found in these rooms, or occasionally the pendulum of life may swing to the other extreme.

You will feel a peculiar harmony and fitness in rooms furnished in your own colors and fewer accidents will occur in such rooms.

If you can have two rooms for your own, furnish each one for your name and the other for your birth digit, and if you can have but one, use your birth digit.

If your name is 11 and your birth 8, choose a 9 vibrating room, as these numbers can not be separated any more than can body, soul and spirit without a disruption of the physical law. One always attends the other.

In furnishing public buildings or hotels, use the colors the rooms vibrate to.

CHAPTER 12

The Colors and the Possibilities of the States, and the Character of the People They Attract

Pythagoras said, "Show me the alphabet of a nation, and I will tell you the character of its people." So we can know the strength of all things by their vibrations, which shows forth as color.

The vowels form the spiritual structure of the alphabet and by their appearance in a name we can read its esoteric possibilities. As man receives his strength from the Divine, so does the earth look to man for its development.

The vibrations of separate states show their possibilities. Their names were not accidents.

The vowels in the name show the kind of people they attract.

In studying the different states and countries keep in mind the Law of Opposites, as taught by Pythagoras and explained in "Success Through Vibration."

Tears and laughter are closely related and both express strong emotions. In the extremes of life, the pendulum may swing past the balance plane to that of high or low vibration. In an instant the shadows may turn to light or the light to darkness, and these extremes create the cyclones of the earth plane, but always a clearing of the mental atmosphere will follow when in the silence the still, small voice is heard.

So we find nations and people with high vibrations clinging to the opposite of what they should represent.

Take as an example Africa. This name vibrates to 11, which stands for the highest visible human advancement. But now it has swung to the dark corner of the vibration. When it turns once more to the light the black will give place to fulfillment.

Its possibilities are great, and when its degradation is removed by the next swing of the pendulum, the people will once more, as they did centuries ago, represent a burning fire of richest red, purple and brown. The country has yellow, violet, black and white covering it like a luminous cloud.

CHAPTER 13

The State That Vibrates 1–Idaho, Michigan, Rhode Island, Connecticut, District of Columbia, North Dakota, Indian Territory

IDAHO

Idaho as a state vibrates 1, Its vowels are i, a, o, = 7. Original ideas will be developed in these subjective states as they vibrate as a whole to 1 or 10 and differ in their physical construction and possibilities as shown by the difference in their vowels. Persons whose name vibrates 1 and birth digit 7 will find something awaiting them in Idaho. It is a good state in which to prepare creative work. By its 9 it will attract the No. 9 people who see everything through the vital, inspirational colors of red from deepest shade to pink.

These people will reap unexpected honors in this subjective state that as a whole vibrates higher than its people.

It will also attract the i's (one') who will either love it devotedly or hate it, as their vibration intensifies the feelings. These ones would do well to go into partnership with a 9 or a 6, as these numbers vibrate more strongly to the objective and can better bring forth the projects No. 1 formulates.

No. 6 will also find plenty of work to employ their busy hands and minds in mothering the products of the earth.

As a whole the people of Idaho will live as if it were the Sunday period of life. It lacks the active 4 vibration.

MICHIGAN

Michigan as a state vibrates 1. Its vowels are i, i, a, also vibrating 1. This state attracts those vibrating red, flame and brown and they make this state a light to attract to the highest in speech and action. Yet their light is in a measure hidden by the fact that state and people vibrate the same esoteric number.

Its prophets will find a better hearing in states that vibrate 8, 9, 11. Those who do not live at their highest in Michigan, will live entirely upon the surface of things.

This, of all states, should be governed by the Law of Unity.

RHODE ISLAND

Rhode Island vibrates 1. Its vowels o, e, i, a, vibrate 3.

It attracts forcibly those whose name digit is 1 and birth digit is 3. These people will find they can concentrate in this state and bring out the latent possibilities of their intellect. 3 is the power of expressing mind and bringing forth hidden treasures.

Its people vibrate to a flame of gold.

CONNECTICUT

Connecticut vibrates 1. Its vowels are o, e, i, u = 5, showing varied points of attraction for those who seek to dwell in the realm of mind.

As a whole the people vibrate to 5, the number of metaphysical research and independent thought in carrying out certain principles. Its strong points of expression are shown in the vowels o and i. These attract inspirational money-makers, also those who have a strong love of state and home.

Principles find a growing favor in this state.

DISTRICT OF COLUMBIA

District of Columbia vibrates 1, the number of Unity and is a principle rather than an objective institution. It calls by its vowels i, i, o, o, u, i, a, to the most refined and conservative of all people the 7's. This is a complete number in limited vibration, and everything these people do, the buildings they construct, the monuments they build, will be likely to be the best of their kind.

District of Columbia calls every class of people except the 5's represented by the vowel e.

The three 9's will be liable to give free expression to the artistic work of the 6's, it is a flame of red, orange, heliotrope and scarlet.

NORTH DAKOTA

North Dakota vibrates 1; Dakota vibrates 7. Why did this state separate from Dakota proper? The people are represented by two kinds of people, only, the o's, the inspirational workers and the 1's, the creators. Dakota is 7, the most conservative of vibrations. It is probable that this progressive, go-ahead people felt bound and hampered when held back by the 7 vibration, so they formed a separate state, and North Dakota will make long strides ahead of the parent state.

INDIAN TERRITORY

Indian vibrates 4 and Territory 6, making 1 as the result of the union of the two classes of workers, the hard workers and the artistic workers.

The people are represented by i, i, a, e, i, o, making 3.

3 always expresses what it finds to express. In this case it must express Unity, and as this idea in a state is a new one to the people of Indian Territory, it is well that there are so many inspirational people among the inhabitants.

The people it calls are of an unusually high class and the state should make giant strides.

It is covered with a flame of red, heliotrope and orange.

CHAPTER 14

The State That Vibrates 2–Nevada

NEVADA

Nevada is the only state in the Union vibrating to the golden-tinted second vibration. Its vowels are e, a, a, = 7.

It calls and attracts those who are journeying through life in the 7 path with a name of 2.

The state vibrates to matter and spirit and the vowels more spirit than matter.

The e shows the realm of mind lingers in the atmosphere of this State and those persons are happiest who yield to its influence, holding always to the power of the absolute.

This state has no middle ground, it has neither white nor black, twilight or dawn.

CHAPTER 15

States That Vibrate 3–Iowa, New York, South Carolina, West Virginia, New Mexico, Arizona

This combination of individual states all vibrate to the expression number 3. This number is the expression of spirit or matter by means of the first Trinity of numbers. It can as easily express 1 as 2, and uses its influence in the way its people desire.

IOWA

Iowa vibrates to 3; its vowels are i, o, a, = 7. It sends out its attractive force to those having the points of contact found in its vowels i, o, a. That is, it attracts the inspirational strong people of 9, as well as those who vibrate 6, scarlet, orange and heliotrope also and the creative flame found in a.

As a whole its people are living in the Sunday of life. They have a tendency to complete a finished work. They are refined and happy, but do not possess the sturdy hard-working activity of the 4 vibration.

NEW YORK

New York vibrates 3; its vowels are e, o, = 11. This state well shows the broad surface the vibration of 3 expresses. It should be a happy meeting place for all kinds of people.

The state of New York calls by its vowels e, o, = 11, for men and women who are vibrating to the highest human vibration, that of the 11. Its people may seek the white light containing all the colors in the gamut of colors, or they may make contact with the darkness and find, like Africa, the abject degradation of a strong vibration. The o shows the objective fascination of all things the e, limited mental aspiration, together developing the strong atmosphere of 11, 3.

SOUTH CAROLINA

South Carolina vibrates to 3. Its vowels are o, u, a, o, i, a, which vibrate as a whole of 8. This state attracts its people by varied lines of vibration from all sources excepting those who vibrate to e, the pink light. This fast vibrating number is absent and its fast revolving character is not felt in South Carolina.

Its people as a whole vibrate to 8, the number of intellect rather than mind, and this leads its successful one into corporations instead of individual work.

These people vibrate to red, purple, brown, scarlet, orange and heliotrope; but as a whole they vibrate to the exclusive color of canary, which is their most successful vibration.

WEST VIRGINIA

West Virginia also vibrates to 3. Its vowels are e, i, i, i, a, = 6. It attracts those persons who vibrate to pink, red, brown and flame and they as a whole show the vibration of 6. This is the rapid vibration of the higher workers, who are money-makers as a whole and inspirational, and yet will not succeed as well as those having more concentrated vibrations.

NEW MEXICO

New Mexico vibrates 3–New 6 and Mexico 6, giving a digit of 3. Its vowels are e, e, i, o, making 7. The state wishes to give expression to 6, the number of the highest class of workers, but the people it calls are living in the day of rest and care more to complete work already begun, than to start new occupations. It will not advance as rapidly as some of the other states.

ARIZONA

Arizona vibrates to 3. Its vowels are a, i, o, a, = 8.
The spiritual structure of Arizona attracts men who

vibrate the free numbers, as its esoteric vibration is higher than the state vibration. All the hidden possibilities of Arizona will be developed by the people it attracts. People of all classes will go to this state and find homes there, yet life will always be dignified and active.

Organized capital will flourish in this state of yellow flame. Its inhabitants cover it with the fine force of yellow and green, making the canary of 8.

ARKANSAS

Arkansas also vibrates 3 and sends out its call to men and women using the 3 force, as shown by its vowels a, a, a. These creative a, o, also resolves into a 3 force. This state and its people lack the gathering or collecting quality found in vibration 2. The inhabitants strike the fundamental principle of creation but its development is weak as shown by its expression.

CHAPTER 16

States That Vibrate 4—Alabama, Mississippi, New Hampshire, North Carolina, Washington, Oklahoma

These states vibrate to the turbulent number 4. Their state colors are blue and green.

These states send out strong physical vibrations of possibilities to those who are able to bear them and all intellectual projects should be successful in a certain limited way.

It is possible for them to express the direct opposite qualities.

ALABAMA

Alabama as a state vibrates to 4. Its vowels also show the same vibration, a, a, a, a, = 4. It sends out only one strong flame of force which is subjective, and by its excess it attracts the opposite to those whose birth or name is the struggling 4 nature.

The state lacks the material principle. It deals with

individual parenthood instead of brotherhood, and yet its people should be of a high vibration, whose strength lies above the physical and intellectual. But in some way they have dropped into the green current and the blue burning above is apt to be unnoticed.

MISSISSIPPI

Mississippi vibrates 4 and is expressed in blue and green.

Its vowels are i, i, i, i, - 9. This state also calls to those who vibrate higher than the state. Weakness is shown in the excess of the high inspirational number of 9. The weakness lies principally in the inharmony of state and people. The state is limited to a hard-working vibration and it calls those only of the inspirational quality, who disregard the demand of the state for hard labor, and this inharmony of vibration will be an obstacle to its progress.

NEW HAMPSHIRE

New Hampshire also vibrates to the active, vigorous, intellectual number 4. Its vowels are e, a, i, e, making 2.

These people vibrate higher than the state and are by nature not as rugged as the state calls for, as the mineral predominating in the bodies of the 2s is gold, a material unfitted for rough labor. It calls those who are philosophical as well as inspirational by the varied vibrations of its vowels e, a, i, e, as a whole resolving themselves into the

2 vibration of gleaners and gatherers of philosophical and inspirational truths.

NORTH CAROLINA

North Carolina as a state vibrates 4, blue and green, and by its vowels attracts through o, a, i, a, the people who vibrate 5, the pink light. It calls to those of varied tones and of great fascination of thought and manners.

WASHINGTON

Washington vibrates to the intellectual and struggling vibration of 4 and its people through the vowels, a, o, i, to the highest vibration, that of the 7. This is a complete number in limited vibration and the people will struggle together until a Moses of free vibration leads them out for the good of the race or for individual gain.

OKLAHOMA

Oklahoma vibrates 4, the hard-working vibration. Life is a struggle in Oklahoma. But it does not call the right people to meets its vigorous vibration. The people are the o's, the high class of workers, and the a's, the creators, which end in 5.

Oklahoma will advance very slowly on account of this inharmony. The fact that the vowels are repeated, intensifies the difference.

CHAPTER 17
The 5 Vibration–Utah

UTAH

Utah is the only state that vibrates 5, of pink color, which mutely asks for love without passion.

The explanation lies in the Law of Opposites, as all countries vibrating 5, in some way, deal with the sex question, the Law of Opposites being Masculine and Feminine.

Its initial letter u, shows its growth will be sustained by the people and the state working in harmony.

It will ever call people of the 4 vibration who will struggle and work for homes and advancement, as the objective 4 people always do. They will rear great cities and build fine homes, but changes are bound to come, as the vowels, u and a, will seek to express a principle which is to them a flame of blue and green.

CHAPTER 18

States That Vibrate 6–Delaware, Massachusetts, Missouri, Montana, Texas, Maine

DELAWARE

Delaware vibrates 6, which stands for maternity, and its vowels call e, a, a, e, = 3. It should mother various projects, but it calls but two classes of people, the intellectual e's and the people with great initiative, the i's. It is possible that the lack of hard-working element may hold back its progress.

MASSACHUSETTS

Massachusetts vibrates to the material vibration of 6. Its vowels are a, a, u, e, = 1. It calls people who are more highly developed to subjective sight than the state. Those whom the state calls desire principles to rule them; they understand the Unity of Life and are stronger upon the unseen than upon the objective side of life.

MISSOURI

Missouri vibrates to 6 and its people are represented by the vowels, i, o, u, i, = 9, a high inspirational people.

There will often be a conflict between state and people, as the people seek the utmost freedom of speech and action and the state will hold them back. Its people will try to express that which is not found and many times when failing to reach the high spiritual law of Universal Brotherhood, they are liable to express the opposite.

It is a state of gorgeous coloring, which if not met, means a barren, colorless life.

MONTANA

Montana, which also vibrates orange, scarlet and heliotrope attracts by its vowels o, a, a, = 8, a different class of people from either Massachusetts, Missouri, or Delaware.

Montana calls for those who belong to the free vibration of 8.

They are people who should organize and bring forth good commercial results. It calls people who will develop everything the state holds by constant attention and care.

As a whole the inhabitants vibrate to canary and to the key of C.

TEXAS

Texas also vibrates 6 and calls to people of the 6th vibration. These people as a whole realize to their fullness the colors of orange, heliotrope and scarlet. They are searchers in the limited vibration of 6. Activity and cheerfulness should be the keynote of Texas, and as the state and people both vibrate to the note of Unity, A, they should make the state a happy, home-like garden, where only moderate labor is required to succeed.

MAINE

Maine vibrates 6, the number of the artistic workers, and the people represented by a, i, e, also vibrate 6.

Among the people it calls are the subjective ones, the people with initiative, the inspirational i's and the people of mind represented by the e's. As from its vibration it is a working state, from the character of the inhabitants a high class of work should be wrought out in Maine.

The people of Maine are distinctly one with the state, as state and people vibrate together. Its greatest strength and weakness lies in this fact.

CHAPTER 19

States That Vibrate 7–California, Dakota, Indiana, Maryland, New Jersey, Tennessee, Wyoming

This group of states vibrates to the vibration of the earth, 7. It is called the finished vibration of the limited cycle. It is the Sunday of weeks and ending of the cycles below it.

These states find a completion in themselves for what is missing of individual comfort. The inhabitants of the group differ, but they must be like the state in some point, or they would not have been attracted within its boundaries. This is true of all the states.

The products of this group of states will always be found equal to the needs of the time.

CALIFORNIA

California attracts by her vowels, a, i, o, i, a those who vibrate the free canary vibration of 8. These people are the highest intellectual type, proud of everything pertaining to their state or family.

They have varied beliefs, as shown by the flame of brown, purple and the different shades of red, and yet as a whole they will make their beliefs conform to the balanced objective and subjective 8. If they err at all, it will be on the side of the material, as their state is an earth bound one.

DAKOTA

Dakota as a state vibrates the same as California, to 7, the people to 8, but the letters show the different manner in which the forces seek expression.

California shows that the harmonious third vibration is found throughout the state by its initial letter of C–3, resolving into the free 8, which shows free expression of its forces.

Dakota's initial letter is D, showing the struggling 4th vibration, which stands for energy and intellectual achievement in contrast to the expression of theories shown in California, which has an inspirational people.

Dakota lacks the element of free expression, but on the other hand is safeguarded by intellectuality against all dangers of inspirational vagaries.

As Dakota people vibrate a, o, a, = 8, higher than the state, they will bring out all the natural advantages to be found in this limited but complete planet-like state.

Its people vibrate to scarlet, heliotrope, and orange with a flame of canary. This state encourages the making of permanent homes and business more strongly than does California.

INDIANA

Indiana vibrates to 7 and has the brick, steel and purple colors.

Its inhabitants, represented by i, i, a, a, are the 2 people, those who gather from all sources and yet are always searchers. The double vowels show them to be inspirational. On the subjective plane they are free, but fail to express the force in objective life. They work in gold color with a flame of red.

They should boldly bring forth their hidden treasure, which they are now holding latent.

MARYLAND

Maryland also vibrates to 7. Her people represented only by the two a's are also two people.

This paucity of vowels shows them to be clannish and conservative. They lie between the numbers that stand for creation and expression and may actualize either or let their powers lie dormant. The people of Maryland live too much in the past–7th vibration–instead of in the actual present.

NEW JERSEY

New Jersey's vibration is 7, showing that it vibrates to all below the limited 7. It, too, will always find everything its inhabitants need. These inhabitants are of the merry, social 6 nature, who in the limited cycle are the highest class of workers. The state vibrates higher than the people it esoterically attracts. It has the maternal quality of 6 and welcomes all guests who come to its shores. Its vowels are only e, e, e, showing inhabitants of one mind, the fascinating but uncertain 5 type. The colors of the people are pink, orange, heliotrope, and scarlet.

TENNESSEE

Tennessee, too, has the 7 vibration of steel and brick and sends out much the same call as New Jersey, except that it goes further into subjective and ends in gold.

Its vowels are only four e's, making the vibration of 2. This represents gold, which is too fine a metal to be put to rough use and when it swings to the opposite extreme finds the opposite of its fine qualities. It has not the same possibilities of many of the other states. The repetition and limitation of the vowels makes too much intensity for use on the objective plane, but should, perhaps, make it rather active in the beginning of the realm of mind. The inhabitants vibrate to gold and pink.

WYOMING

Wyoming vibrates 7 and the people to the same digit as New Jersey, 6, but they are totally different kind of people.

New Jersey's force is in a manner lost in the state, as it contains nothing but three e's. Wyoming's vowels are o, i, and its esoteric strength lies in the o, which pushes out for expression and seeks to bring forth ever possibility the state holds.

The colors of the state are steel and brick; of the people, orange, scarlet and heliotrope.

CHAPTER 20

States That Vibrate 8–Georgia, Nebraska, Pennsylvania, Vermont, Virginia, Wisconsin

These states vibrate to the free and unlimited number of 8. Their color is canary.

In these states fortunes may be made and lost with greater ease than in states that show a limited vibration. There is an air of freedom which seems to spring from the streams and mountains to urge men to great undertakings.

In this group of states, if men will remember their brother's rights, unlimited power and money will be gained without the amount of service labor necessary in the states of limited vibrations.

GEORGIA

Georgia vibrates 8 and yields the composite colors composing canary. It is a flame of yellow, green and white which composes this color. The vowels are e, o, i, a, making the vibration of 3. This number expresses what it comes in contact with. In this case it must represent canary, pink, scarlet, orange, heliotrope and red, and the a makes a binding flame, which should make for strength.

Persons vibrating 8, 9, 11 or 22, should succeed in Georgia, provided they keep steadfastly in mind the idea of the Brotherhood of Man.

NEBRASKA

Nebraska vibrates 8, but its people will not take advantage of all their opportunities as they are represented by the vowels, e, a, a, making the conservative people 7, who can not understand the great possibilities of the State. If they would cease living in the Sabbath of life, they would find they have hidden strength and could bring it forth as 8, 9, 11, 22.

PENNSYLVANIA

Pennsylvania also vibrates 8, the canary color, and attracts people of the 7 vibration, who as a class are too conservative to get the full value from the state; the people vibrate lower than the state.

These people, however, have the advantage over the Nebraskans, as the vowels are stronger and more varied, e, a, i, a, making 7 but containing the free 9 of inspiration, which calls individual giants to its borders.

It has great hidden strength and will continue to burn as a flame, always going ahead under the lead of the giants who continually urge their fellow countrymen to leave their exclusiveness and come out of the Sunday life.

The 8 vibration, mingling with the 7 of Nebraska and Pennsylvania, make them places for the development of religious sects.

VERMONT

Vermont vibrates 8 as a state, the color of canary, but its hidden strength lies with the people who vibrate to the very highest e, o, making 11 and holding the force of black, white, yellow and violet. Had this state a 9 among its numbers, it would be a very giant of strength. As it is, it sadly lacks the power to express the human quality.

The 8 of the state stands for intellectuality and advancement; the true 11 of its people caring nothing for expression and hiding their strength. The unexpected may occur at any time in Vermont.

VIRGINIA

Virginia also vibrates 8, the canary color. It attracts as its inhabitants i, i, i, a, vibrating to the limited and unlimited i. Its esoteric value is revealed by the three i's of all numbers denoting the fullest expression of soul, as revealed in the vital red of the 9.

Mingled with the 8 the people show pride in land.
The brown lends depth to the inspiration of the reds.
The people will ever lead the state of Virginia.

WISCONSIN

Wisconsin also vibrates to the canary of 8. By its vowels i, o, i, it attracts the 6 vibration of people. It is more physical than the state of Virginia, as the 6 steps out boldly with its inspiration and discoveries and expects the world to recognize what it offers.

In organization and mining interests, the state as a whole will lead its people.

CHAPTER 21
States That Vibrate 9–Alaska, Illinois

Alaska and Illinois vibrate to the strong, free vibration of 9–the vibration that holds the rich colors of red and brown. These individual states hold great wealth, both of a material and spiritual kind and are to be felt as powers.

ALASKA

Alaska's esoteric value lies in the creative force of the three a's, a, a, a, making 3. This 3 vibration reproduces or expresses the 9 of the state and causes its inhabitants to feel as one with the state. Like all the other 9 combination, Alaska will attract people vibrating 8, 9, 11, 22. These people will find great possibilities to develop in this state and, notwithstanding the climate, will so strongly feel the attractive force of the state that they will be loath to leave it.

ILLINOIS

Illinois vibrates to the free 9 and its spiritual structure is of such a nature it reproduces its own atmosphere in its people, as shown by its vowels, i, i, o, i, making the 6th vibration. As this vibration expresses the maternal quality, it fosters the growth of all important thought and the three i's, which have physical strength, give it material expression.

The state vibrates to red, and with it the people being orange, which calls for power, scarlet, the vivid surging of physical life, and heliotrope, which expresses the freedom of the plane above the material. They are emotional people, strong for good or evil; this strong state vibrates higher than its people.

CHAPTER 22
States That Vibrate 11–Florida, Kansas, Kentucky, Louisiana, Minnesota, Ohio, Oregon, Colorado

This group of states vibrates to the highest of human vibration, 11–the one number no man can define, as its possibilities are unlimited in all directions. It is the number of the greatest and the smallest, having very little middle ground. These states vibrate to black, white, yellow and violet. Everything for the good of the body, soul and spirit should be found in the 11 vibration. These states differ, as do individuals, in personal characteristics, but in strength all of them are powers.

FLORIDA

Florida vibrates to 11 and calls to people of the o, i, a, the 7th vibration or to the limited numbers beneath 7. It sends its call to this refined but conservative people, who are holding back the state, which stands for unlimited freedom in all things.

Its spiritual structure, represented by the inhabitants, stays the hand of the unlimited, as the conservative 7's fear the ban of lawless thought and hold the state to the finished vibration of 7. The people as a whole vibrate to brick and steel, but there are people there who vibrate to o and also to i, showing that the creative flame of red, scarlet, orange and heliotrope is felt in the atmosphere.

KANSAS

Kansas, too, vibrates 11, but attracts a different class of people. The vowels are a, a, a double flame of creative light, expressing a people of hidden spiritual principles, who show very little of the physical. The state vibrates to the highest spiritual vibration and the people lack but one vibration of making the same. If it had more of the objective element, its ideals should be more easily realized. As it is, its colors are too fine to move the earth currents as they would if it had something beside "a" in its structure.

To succeed, Kansas must ever hold fast to its ideals; otherwise like Africa, it will swing to the dark side of its vibration and the blackness of gloom will pervade it. It is a free lamp of spirit, burning for the Creator.

KENTUCKY

Kentucky vibrates 11. Its vowels are e, u, = 8. Its colors are the white, black, yellow, and violet of 11, the canary of 8 and the pink of e, all of the most refined order. They show vibrations of spiritualized love, the psychic sense and rest. The white shows realized ideals, the black those of the unrealized. The canary shows a material freedom of the body, which is expressed sometimes in intellectual haughtiness; its ideals are the highest, and if they are not lived the opposite will be expressed.

Kentucky calls people of only two kinds, while Kansas calls for but one kind of people. Others may come, but their roots will not sink deep into the soil.

LOUISIANA

Louisiana vibrates to 11 and has the blessings or the darkness of this high vibration. Its spiritual structure, unlike Kansas and Kentucky, calls many kinds of people to its borders, as shown by its vowels, o, u. i, i, a, a, = 11.

It looks as if it might have begun as a money-making state, o, then gone into an inspirational period, i, i; later on it will go into a subjective condition, and as a shows ideals of the highest or the lowest and the state and people vibrate 11, the people will appear in parts as lamps of shining light, sitting in the high place of the temple. The vibrations of this state are varied, but over all is the unborn freedom of the 11, which any of its inhabitants can use, or they may sink into the gloom of unrealized desires.

MINNESOTA

Minnesota vibrates 11 and calls to people through black, white, yellow, and violet, and its call is answered by a varied people, as shown in the vowels i, e, o, u, ending in the vibration of 3. This 3 mentally asks the people to vibrate with the state in the high 11. This state calls to many different kinds of minds and offers freedom to all those who live at their highest.

OHIO

Ohio vibrates 11 and calls to people through o, i, o, giving the digit of 3. These vowels by their structure give a balance of the objective to the state and people. The state vibrates the highest of all vibrations, and its people are the highest type of inspirational workers. As the state vibrates higher than its people, in this case, this gives an element of security.

The 3 people are the highest expression of the Trinity of Mind, and as the state sends out vibrations of the highest quality of spirit and matter, Ohio is a strong, safe state, whose people see beyond the range of material things.

OREGON

Oregon vibrates 11 and its spiritual structure is shown in o, e, o, = 8. As the vowels are all those of limited vibration, it attracts those who are individually less strong than those of Ohio, but as a whole they form into the strong free number of canary, the 8. This strong free number, together with the spirit of freedom given by the state, will cause the people to develop higher vibrations. The state has bright prospects, providing it does not turn into the darkness.

COLORADO

Colorado also vibrates 11 and its spiritual structure is shown in o, o, a, o. The wealth of the vowel o, give it the human quality needed when the people vibrate to 1.

This number calls for the unity of wealth, making o's to hold its people to the state, which vibrates a little higher than its inhabitants.

Colorado must succeed, as her people will uphold the unity of the state as shown by the 1, which is the hidden flame, showing upon the surface in orange, scarlet and heliotrope.

UNITED STATES

Officially the title of our country is The United States of America, which vibrates to the pivotal number of the soul, the free vibration of 9 in the trinity of Body, Soul and Spirit.

This is the plane where free expression in its highest form should come forth into objective life.

The name by which we are commonly known, The United States, vibrates to the subjective number of Unity as expressed in the vibration of 1; its vowels or spiritual structure also calls the 1's of high creative power to its shores.

It could not be the home it is for all classes of men were this high vibration the one in actual use and the only one in force, but the free expression number 9 calls for all classes, those of limited and unlimited development.

The esoteric value of the full title is e, u, i, e, a, e, o, a, e, i, a, = 5.

This combination contains all the vowels, so the call is to all kinds and conditions of men who flock to our shores and find their average in 5, the number which gives versatility and a reaching out of independent mind and thought.

The country will ever be a soul home for those who are reaching out above the ordinary plane of life.

The esoteric value of the name in common use, The United States, is represented by e, u, i, e, a, e, = 1, the same high vibration as the country that calls them. These people are subjective and original.

Like Greece of old, the country sends out a triple call to the eager e's.

The United States calls all classes except the artistic workers, the 6's. This may be why we have so far fallen a little short in original artistic work; but as these people also are called in the official title, which is in a manner held dormant, even their work can be brought out into objective life.

The United States and the people who represent it stand for unity. All of these eager searching e's are ready to sink their own individuality in the one paramount idea of unity. That is the one great idea for which the United States stands,–a unity that will bind her people of all nations together as one people, and which will express itself individually as a perfect union of Body, Soul, and Spirit.

CHAPTER 23

Our Island Possessions

PUERTO RICO

Porto Rico expresses herself by 3, 9, making a digit of 3. The vowels are o, o, i, o, of the numerical value of 9. This calls strong, free, loving men to its shores, who will express all the possibilities of the island.

It was formerly known as Puerto Rico of the 5 vibration. Its vowels then were u, e, o, i, o, making 11. This change was not accidental. When the United States first took possession, Congress decreed that the name should be known as Puerto Rico–5, esoteric value 11. But in a few months, without any explanation being given, it was changed to Porto Rico, 3 esoteric value 9.

The free 9 being present in Rico, as Puerto Rico it probably gave too free expression to the sex element (5) and thereby caused confusion, which the inhabitants were unable to meet, as the inclination would be to linger in the dark side of the 11, when they were not able to reach its height. Whatever the cause, the name was changed to Porto Rico, which in Spanish is absolutely meaningless; but with this name the country has many possibilities. Its greater danger lies in the people giving themselves too freely to the pleasure loving vibration of the 9; this vibration also possesses the tendency to develop feuds, which will be given free expression.

The island, and its people, belong to the free, happy vibration of red and all its shades, with orange and heliotrope. It lacks the coordination of the canary and cream found in the even numbers.

THE PHILIPPINES

The Philippines vibrate to 7, and like all others of the highest limited vibration, it will ever resent the interference of other vibrations.

Its vowels are i, i, i, e. It has too many high vibrating i's for any one to reach and find its digit or level in the limited number 5, showing its people will ever desire lawless freedom, reaching as a whole the changing plane of 5. Yet this country will ever be an interesting and fascinating one, showing a kind of refinement even its crude desires for advancement.

HAWAII

Hawaii vibrates 6, the number of the highest workers, and its inhabitants have the numerical value 2. It calls a, a, i, i to the inspirational free 9's and to the subjective i's.

There will be a great deal of work done in Hawaii, but the danger will be that island and people will not rise above the material. In this case the inhabitants will not be comfortable and will probably leave the island in disgust without being able to give a good reason for their dissatisfaction.

Its colors are scarlet, heliotrope, orange and gold.

CHAPTER 24

To Find The Character of
Different Parts of Cities or States

PHILADELPHIA

As countries differ in topography and climate, so do they differ in vibration, and different cities and different parts of the same city attract residents of similar tastes. This is brought about by the natural law of vibration. North, South, East and West vibrate to different expressions of that law.

North vibrates 3,

South vibrates 2,

East vibrates 9,

West vibrates 4,

The vowel of North is o, = 6.

The vowels of South are o, u, = 9.

The vowels of East are e, a, = 6.

The vowel of West is e, = 5.

Philadelphia vibrates to 11. Its vowels i, a, e, i, a, = 7.

Pennsylvania vibrates to 11. Its vowels are i, a, e, i, a, = 7.

Philadelphia, Pennsylvania, vibrate to 11, 8, and will ever possess a freedom and standing not comprehended by the people it attracts. The spiritual structure of both Philadelphia and of Pennsylvania is 7, the vibration of a complete planet in limited vibration. Philadelphia will ever remain in the refined Sunday atmosphere of life, the inhabitants complete in themselves, like the vibration which calls them.

This is true as a whole, but different sections call those with similar tastes to different parts, as North Philadelphia, South Philadelphia, West Philadelphia, and the eastern part.

North Philadelphia vibrates 3, 11. They will re-express the city as it is, only in a more material way, its vowel being the maternal 6, which holds the many colors which express the many forces lying back of it.

They are a gay, happy people, who will make homes which they will enjoy for themselves. The 7 of Philadelphia added to their own 6 makes them the energetic 4. These people will build and make homes for posterity.

SOUTH PHILADELPHIA

South Philadelphia calls another class of people by its vowels, o, u, those of the free 9 vibration. The city vibrates to 11 and South to 2, making 2, 11. This is inexpressive unless combined with 3, 6, or 9. The 2 vibration draws and holds its own treasure. The 9 of their vowels is the free vibration of mind. These people should be heeded in matters concerning the city, because they have the unlimited mental vision which can see beyond the present. When disagreeing with North Philadelphia, they feel the fetter of the limited 6, making often their own 9 fall to the lower number. The 6 people have glimpses of ideal life, which South Philadelphia should bring into objective life.

WEST PHILADELPHIA

West Philadelphia vibrates to the energetic, limited number 4. Its vowel is e, of the numerical value of 5. The people are distinctly divided from the plane of their section; 4 desires to build, to win, to save, and believes nothing that it can not see with the outward eye; and the subjective 5 is in direct conflict.

This part of Philadelphia will be the section where occult science will take root–as it vibrates to the limited realm of mind. Its people vibrate to pink and the section to green and blue.

EAST PHILADELPHIA

East Philadelphia vibrates to the free 9, 11. This part of the city which has had free expression and calls all humanity to its ports. It should be, and is the business part of the city. The vowels are e, a, = 6. The people are those with initiative who will put their ideas into force, being the highest class of workers.

The variety of forces is shown in the varied colors, scarlet, orange and heliotrope. Their esoteric value added to their 7 of the whole makes them the energetic 4 people–most of the workers are probably in North and East Philadelphia.

New Falcon Publications
**Publisher of Controversial Books and CDs
Invites You to Visit Our Website:
http://www.newfalcon.com**

At the Falcon website you can:

- Browse the online catalog of all our great titles, including books by Robert Anton Wilson, Christopher S. Hyatt, Israel Regardie, Aleister Crowley, Timothy Leary, Osho, Lon Milo DuQuette and many more
- Find out what's available and what's out of stock
- Get special discounts
- Order our titles through our secure online server
- Find products not available anywhere else including:
    – One of a kind and limited availability products
    – Special packages
    – Special pricing
- And much, much more

Get online today at http://www.newfalcon.com